A Ticket to

Brazil

Elizabeth Weitzman

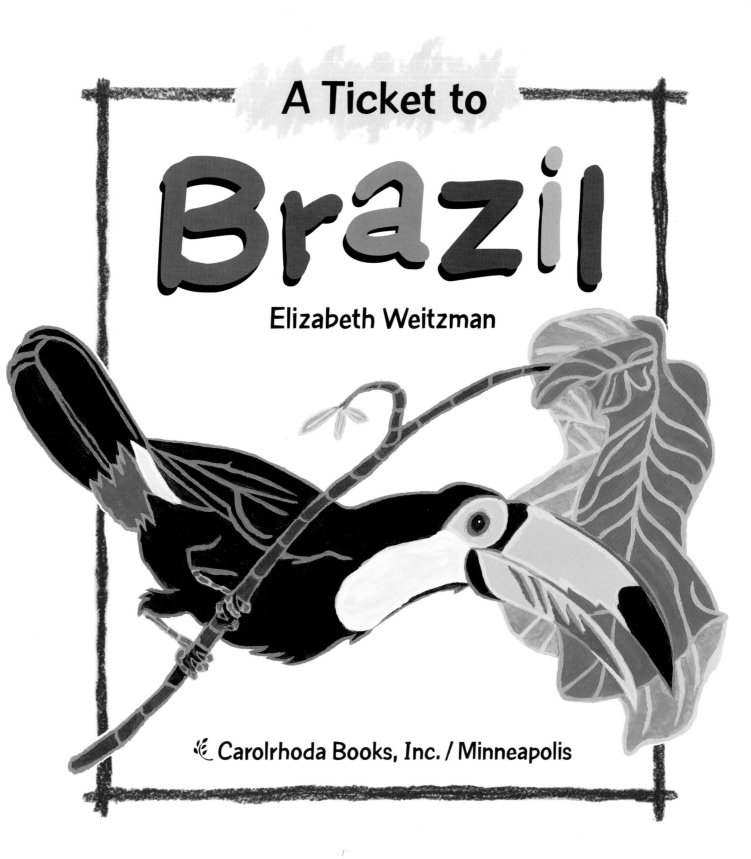

Carolrhoda Books, Inc. / Minneapolis

Photo Acknowledgments

Photographs, maps, and artworks are used courtesy of: John Erste, pp. 1, 2−3, 11, 21, 27, 30−31, 39; Laura Westlund, pp. 4, 15; © SuperStock, Inc., pp. 6 (left), 10 (left); © Michele Burgess, pp. 6−7, 8, 24 (left); D. Donne Bryant Stock: (© Juca Martins) pp. 7, 19 (right), (© Craig Duncan) p. 9 (top), (© Nair Benedicto) pp. 9 (bottom), 11, 13, 25, 40, (© Stefan Kolumban) p. 16, (© Robert Fried) pp. 18, 26, (© Michael Moody) p. 19 (left), (© Ricardo Teles) p. 27, (© Mauricio Simonetti) pp. 29, 34, (© Vince DeWitt) p. 35 (top); Visuals Unlimited: (© Erwin C. "Bud" Nielsen) p. 10 (bottom right), (© Beth Davidow) p.22 (right); © Buddy Mays/TRAVEL STOCK, pp. 10 (top right); © Sue Cunningham/SCP, pp. 12, 23 (bottom), 31, 36, 37 (both), 38, 42, 43 (both); © Wolfgang Kaehler, pp. 14, 22 (left), 33 (left), 45; © Mary Altier, pp. 15 (bottom), 21, 41; © TOM STACK & ASSOCIATES: (© Byron Augustin) pp. 15 (top), 32; TRIP: (© M. Barlow) pp. 17, 23 (right), (© R. Belbin) p. 24 (right), (© D. Harding) p. 28, (© S. Grant) p. 33 (right), (© Eric Smith) p. 44; © Bettmann, p. 35 (bottom). Cover photo © Buddy Mays/TRAVEL STOCK.

Copyright © 1998 by Elizabeth Weitzman

Carolrhoda Books, Inc.
c/o The Lerner Publishing Group
241 First Avenue North
Minneapolis, Minnesota 55401 U.S.A.

Website address: www.lernerbooks.com

Library of Congress Cataloging-in-Publication Data

Weitzman, Elizabeth,
    Brazil / by Elizabeth Weitzman.
      p.   cm. — (A ticket to)
    Includes index.
    Summary: An introduction to the geography, history, economy, culture, and people of Brazil.
      ISBN 1−57505−132−X (lib. bdg. : alk. paper)
      1. Brazil—Juvenile literature. [1. Brazil.] I. Title.
    II. Series:
    F2508.5.W45   1998
    981—dc 21   97−43714

Mauufactured in the United States of America
1 2 3 4 5 6 − JR − 03 02 01 00 99 98

Contents

Welcome! 5

The Land 6

A Hot Time! 8

The Amazon 10

The First Brazilians 12

A Mix of People 14

Rich and Poor 16

Foods from Brazil 18

Let's Talk! 20

Getting Around 22

Religion 24

Music 26

Carnaval 28

Festivals 30

School 32

Sports 34

Television 36

Let's Eat! 38

Families 40

Arts and Crafts 42

New Words to Learn 44

New Words to Say 46

More Books to Read 47

New Words to Find 48

Welcome!

In the year 1500, Portuguese sailors landed in what became one of the biggest countries in the world—Brazil. This huge land takes up almost half of the **continent** of South America. Brazil's eastern edge stretches along the Atlantic Ocean. Brazil's other borders touch almost every nation in South America.

Map Whiz Quiz

Trace the map of Brazil (left) onto a piece of paper. Look for the Atlantic Ocean. Mark this side of your map with an "E" for east. How about Peru? Mark this side with a "W" for west. Now look for Brasília—the capital of Brazil. Color the capital star red. Next color in the Amazon rain forest. How much of Brazil does the forest take up?

The busy city of São Paulo

The Land

The long Amazon River flows across northern Brazil. A huge **tropical rain forest** grows here, too.

Farmers raise crops in northeastern Brazil. Farther inland is a dry, hilly area called the backlands. But watch your step! Cactuses and prickly shrubs are everywhere.

Iguaçu Falls is one of the most beautiful places in Brazil.

Brazil's biggest cities, Rio de Janeiro and São Paulo, lie along the Atlantic coast in southern Brazil. Also in the south are big farms, rolling grasslands, and the Iguaçu Falls.

At least 2,000 kinds of animals live in the swamplands of southwestern Brazil. This huge **swamp** is home to alligators, boa constrictors, otters, and jabiru birds.

A jabiru bird

A Hot Time!

If you visit Brazil in December, leave your coat at home! It is summer there, and it is *really* hot! Summer in Brazil starts in December and lasts until March. Winter lasts from June until August.

Brazil does not get much snow. But when it rains in the Amazon forest, it pours. Central Brazil

When the weather is hot, Brazilian kids love to cool off in the Atlantic Ocean.

A lot of rain keeps the Amazon rain forest (above) *leafy and green. But droughts in central Brazil* (left) *leave the soil dry and cracked.*

Upside Down

Do you know why Brazil's seasons are the opposite of ours? It is because Brazil lies south of the **equator.** Countries in this part of the world have winter when we have summer. And they have summer when we have winter. If you are wearing your bathing suit at the beach in June, what do you think a Brazilian kid would be wearing?

hardly gets any rain at all. **Droughts** (times of dry weather) may last for two years.

The mighty Amazon!

A colorful toucan

A squirrel monkey

The Amazon

The Amazon River is the second longest river in the world. And the Amazon forest has thousands of animals. There are anteaters, monkeys, toucans, and tons of insects.

10

The Amazon rain forest is in trouble. Mining, farming, and logging companies want to use the land. They are cutting down trees and polluting the waters. These actions hurt the animals and plants in the Amazon.

Some trees in the Amazon rain forest can grow 165 feet into the sky—that is as tall as a 20-story building.

Some Brazilians are burning the rain forest to create farmland.

The First Brazilians

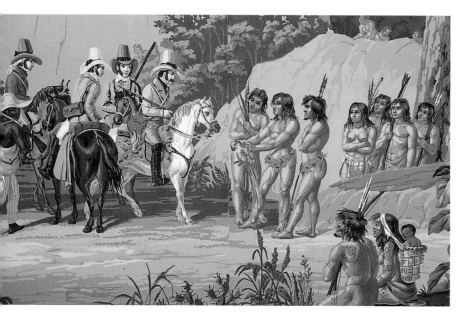

Native peoples greeted the Portuguese when they first came to Brazil. Later the first Brazilians and the Portuguese did not get along.

Long ago millions of native peoples (or Indians) lived in Brazil. Then the Portuguese came. They forced Indians to work as slaves. Many of the Indians died from sickness and from too much hard work. Other Indians escaped into the Amazon forest.

These days some Indians live in Brazil's cities. Others have homes far from towns. The Yanomami live in the Amazon rain forest.

The Kaiapo Indians are among the 200 Indian groups that still live in Brazil.

They hunt for food with bows and arrows. Another Amazon group called the Txucarramae paint their bodies for special ceremonies.

A Mix of People

More than 160 million people live in Brazil. Many Brazilians come from mixed backgrounds. Some have African and Indian parents and grandparents. Others claim European and Indian backgrounds. Still others have European and African family members.

The Portuguese brought Africans to Brazil as slaves long ago. These days slavery is against the law in Brazil. But the Africans who stayed shared their food, music, and religions.

Brazilian schoolgirls make faces for the camera.

No Touching!

In the old days, African slaves in Brazil were punished for fighting. So they came up with *capoeira*— a type of fighting that looks like dancing. Capoeira performers spin and kick to the beat of drums and an instrument called a *berimbau*.

Dear Grandma and Grandpa:

Yesterday we arrived in Salvador It is really neat here! The streets are steep and curvy. The houses are painted different colors, like pink, green, and yellow. Mom says that many of the people who live here are African Brazilians. Some of the women wear African-style clothes. They wrap pretty scarves around their heads. They also wear long skirts and shirts made of lace. Mom bought me some wooden beads that are just like the ones these women wear. Gotta go—it's time for lunch!

Rich and Poor

Brazil has very rich people and many poor people. The wealthy people often live in big homes. They have cooks to prepare their meals and maids to do the

Many poor people in Brazil's cities live in shacks made of cardboard, wood, and tin.

housework. The adults have good jobs. Their kids go to good schools.

Many poor people in big cities live in slums called *favelas*. Their homes are made of

Breathing Room

Brazilians are crowded together in the cities. But in the countryside, they live miles away from one another. In the grasslands of southern Brazil, a kid could leave the family farm and walk for two days without running into anybody else (except for a couple of cows).

cardboard, wood, and tin. A lot of the favela homes do not have lights, running water, or indoor toilets.

Many of the children from the favelas do not go to school. They spend their days begging. Some do not have families and have nowhere to sleep at night.

Vendors in the city of Salvador sell many colorful fruits and vegetables. Can you name any of these foods?

Foods from Brazil

Did you know that Brazil's farms grow much of the world's oranges, coffee, and wheat? So if you drink orange juice for breakfast, the oranges may have come from Brazil. Did you have a hamburger for dinner last night? The beef in your burger might have come from a Brazilian cattle ranch.

Some of the workers on Brazil's ranches are called gauchos, or cowboys. These men wear big hats, wide pants, and capes called ponchos.

Coffee pickers (above) *and gauchos* (left) *are Brazilian farmworkers.*

Many farmworkers in Brazil live right on the farm. Workers who do not live on the farm are called *boias frias* (meaning "cold meal") because they carry a bag lunch to work every day.

Let's Talk!

Most people in Brazil speak Portuguese. But Brazil has lots of people from other lands. They sometimes speak their languages, such as Japanese or Italian, at home. Native peoples in Brazil have their own languages, too. Brazilian Indians called the Tupí-Guaraní gave us the words *jaguar* and *tapioca*.

Counting

Here's how to count to 10 in Portuguese.

English	Portuguese
one	*um* (OONG)
two	*dois* (DOH-eez)
three	*três* (TRAYS)
four	*quatro* (KWAH-troo)
five	*cinco* (SEEN-koo)
six	*seis* (SAY-ees)
seven	*sete* (SEHT-chee)
eight	*oito* (OY-too)
nine	*nove* (NOH-vee)
ten	*dez* (DEHZ)

This sign says, "we have coco gelado" in Portuguese. Coco gelado is a special Brazilian treat—an ice-cold coconut with the top cut off. Just stick in a straw and drink up!

Getting Around

Brazilians go places in lots of different ways. People from the Amazon region usually climb into a canoe. Rich people often fly from one place to another.

In the cities, traffic is crazy. Lots of people drive cars.

In the Amazon, most people travel by canoe (left) or by ferry (above). The Amazon River is like a highway for boats!

Beep Beep! Avenida Presidente Vargas (left) *is a wide street in Rio de Janeiro. The street has 10 lanes for cars—and it still has traffic jams! Many people in Rio use trolley cars* (below).

Other people squeeze onto crowded buses, subways, and trolley cars. So look both ways—twice!—before you cross the street in Brazil.

This Catholic church is in Salvador (above).

An African Brazilian Spiritualist (below)

Religion

The Portuguese brought the Roman Catholic religion to Brazil. Most Brazilians are Catholics. Other Brazilians practice **Spiritualism.** For example, many Indian peoples believe in nature spirits and in the spirits of their dead family members.

24

Sink or Swim?

Many Brazilians honor the African sea goddess Iêmanjá. On New Year's Eve, worshipers dress in white and go to a river or to the ocean to offer her flowers. The goddess likes the way she looks. So people also bring her combs, mirrors, and makeup. If the gifts sink, it means Iêmanjá is pleased. She will grant the giver's wishes. If the gifts float back to shore, her worshipers had better try a little harder!

A lot of African Brazilian Spiritualists pray to gods and goddesses.

Samba musicians in Brazil are known as sambistas.

Music

Brazilians play all kinds of music. The
lambada is a mix of music from the Amazon
region and from islands in the Caribbean
Sea. The samba mixes **Latin American**
and African beats.

Brazilian country music tells stories of love, of hard work, and of life in small towns.

Brazilians love making and listening to music.

Make a Maraca

Brazilian kids make maracas out of a dried vegetable called a gourd. Gourds have rattling beans inside. You can make a maraca with stuff you have at home. Fill one plastic egg or a small cardboard box about the size of your hand with 10 dried beans. Tightly tape the two halves of the egg together. If you are using a box, tape it shut. Decorate your maraca with magic markers, glitter, stickers, and anything else you can find. Then shake!

What an outfit! This woman is all decked out for Carnaval.

Question

Can you think of a U.S. city that has a similar carnival celebration every year?

(New Orleans)

Carnaval

Everybody takes part in Carnaval (or Carnival)—Brazil's greatest celebration. Carnaval happens in February or March. Schools and offices shut down for four days of dancing, music, parties, and parades.

People make dazzling costumes and huge floats. They march down the street through streams of confetti and cheering crowds.

People in Rio de Janeiro watch Carnaval festivities from a huge viewing stand called the Sambodromo.

Festivals

Many Brazilian kids say June is their favorite month because of the *festas juninhas,* or June festivals. These festivals celebrate several saints. During this month, people have barbecues, dances, and all-night bonfires. Children send colorful balloons into the air and watch fireworks after dark.

Bonfim Bracelets

In Salvador people enjoy the Festival do Bonfim in January. For good luck, people exchange Bonfim bracelets. They tie a single ribbon in knots around a friend's wrist. For each knot, the wearer gets one wish. When the ribbon wears out and breaks, the wishes come true. But you cannot tie your own bracelet. The ribbon has to be a gift.

Brazilian Festivals

There are so many festas *(festivals) in Brazil, it is hard to find a week without one!*

January 1 New Year's Day

February (week before Lent) Carnaval

March or April Good Friday

May 1 Labor Day

May or June Corpus Christi

June (all month) Festas Juninhas

September 7 Independence Day

October 12 Nossa Senhora de Aparecida (honors Brazil's patron saint)

November 2 All Souls Day

December 25 Christmas

December 31 New Year's Eve

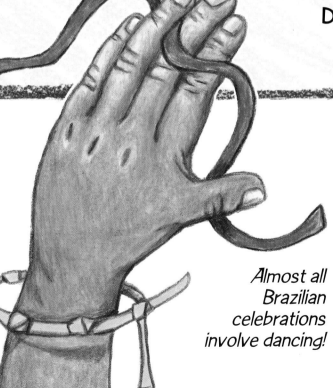

Almost all Brazilian celebrations involve dancing!

School

A young Brazilian pays attention in class.

Brazilian kids go to primary school from the time they are 6 until they are 13 or 14. Every year students have to take a big test. If they pass, they can move up to the next grade. But if they fail, they have to repeat the year. And guess what? School vacation lasts from January to March. (Remember, that is their summer.)

Some parents do not have enough money to buy school uniforms and books for their children.

This young Brazilian is selling candy. He will use the money to help support his family.

A one-room school in the Amazon region

Or the nearest school might be very far away. So lots of kids do not go to school. They never learn to read or write.

33

Sports

Brazilians love to play soccer. Brazilian kids learn the sport when they are very young. Brazilians also like to play basketball (facing page).

Brazilians love *futebol.* That is the Portuguese word for soccer. Every big city has a futebol stadium. Maracanã Stadium in Rio can pack in 180,000 fans. These fans go wild at every match. They paint themselves in their team colors and scream at every goal.

They all hope their team will go to the World Cup. This is the world's biggest soccer match. It takes place every four years.

A Soccer Hero

Pelé (Edson Arantes do Nascimento) was only 16 years old when he helped Brazil win the World Cup in 1958. He is the only player to ever score more than 1,000 goals in his career. He is one of the world's most famous sports heroes.

Xuxa

Television

Kids in Brazil spend a lot of time outside. But they also like to watch TV. Kids all over the country love to watch Xuxa. She is the host of children's TV shows in Brazil. These shows feature music, dancing, games, and big, loud audiences filled with kids.

Brazilian adults are glued to their TVs when a *novela* is on. These TV soap operas are on every night but Sunday.

Brazilians of all ages love to watch television.

Not everyone in the countryside has a television. So friends and neighbors may watch together.

Brazilians are not the only ones who love these shows. They are translated into Spanish so people in other Latin American countries can watch, too.

Looks delicious! Feijoada *served with rice, orange slices, and kale makes a colorful and tasty meal.*

Let's Eat!

The most popular dish in Brazil is probably *feijoada.* This stew is made with black beans and meat. Feijoada is served with white rice, orange slices, and a green vegetable named kale. Cooks also serve *farofa* with this dish. Farofa is a toasted flour made from a starchy root called manioc.

Brazilian Fruits

A lot of different kinds of fruits grow in Brazil. Next time you go to the grocery store, look for bananas, oranges, star fruit, passion fruit, mangoes, strawberries, melons, and apples from Brazil.

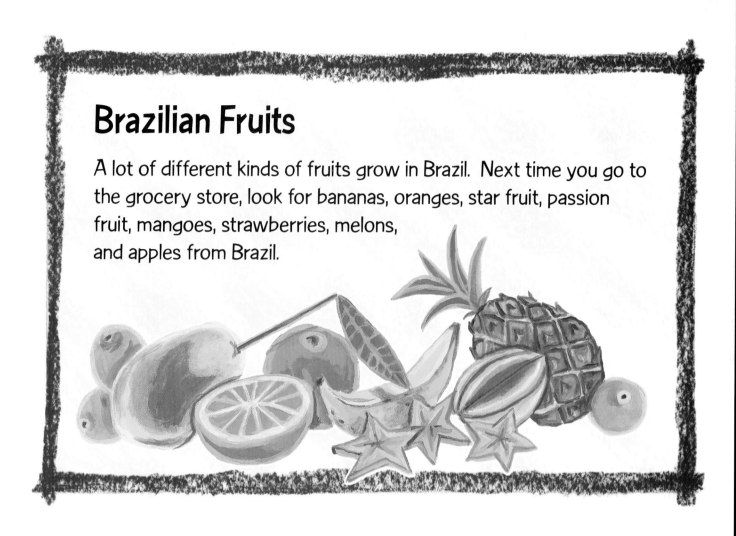

African Brazilian cooks use coconut milk and spicy chili peppers. On Brazilian ranches, meat is popular. There are more than 2,500 kinds of fish in the Amazon region. I bet you can guess what most people eat there!

Families

Families in Brazil are often very large. They may have five, six, or more kids. Grandparents usually live with or near their children. And do not forget godparents. They are close to their godchildren and are almost a part of the family.

A Brazilian family sits down for a meal.

All in the Family

Practice these Portuguese words with your family.

grandfather	avô	(ah-VOH)
grandmother	avó	(ah-VAW)
father	pai	(PY)
mother	mãe	(MY)
uncle	tio	(TEE-oo)
aunt	tia	(TEE-ah)
son	filho	(FEEL-yoo)
daughter	filha	(FEEL-yah)
brother	irmão	(eeh-MOW^n)
sister	irmã	(eeh-MAH^n)

Brazilians are very affectionate. If you visit a family, everybody will hug you or kiss you on both cheeks.

Brazilian weavers made this colorful rug.

Arts and Crafts

Brazilians make many different kinds of crafts. In southern Brazil, people weave beautiful rugs with pictures of houses and churches. You can put these rugs on the floor or hang them on the wall.

Northeastern Brazil is known for its hammocks. Brazilian potters make yellow pottery with clay that comes from southeastern Brazil. They make red pottery with clay that comes from northeastern Brazil.

Artists in the town of Santarém made these two tall pots (above). *Hammocks* (right) *are sort of like swinging couches.*

Gigantic water lillies float on the Amazon River.

New Words to Learn

continent: Any one of seven large areas of land. The world's continents are Africa, Antarctica, Asia, Australia, Europe, North America, and South America.

drought: A long period of dry weather without rain or snow.

equator: The line that circles a globe's middle section halfway between the North Pole and the South Pole.

Latin America: The parts of North and South America lying to the south of the United States that were settled by Spaniards. Latin America also includes Brazil.

The furry three-toed sloth lives in the Amazon.

Spiritualism: A religion whose followers believe in and pray to spirits. The spirits may be related to animals, nature, or the ancestors of living people.

swamp: An area of land that is soaked with water. Trees, shrubs, and other woody plants are the main forms of plant life in a swamp.

tropical rain forest: A thick, green forest that gets lots of rain every year. These forests lie in the hot regions of the world near the equator.

New Words to Say

Bahia	bah-EE-uh
berimbau	beh-ree^n-BOW
boias frias	BOH-ahs FREE-ahs
Brasília	brah-ZEEL-yuh
capoeira	kah-PWAY-rah
coco gelado	KOH-koo zheh-LAH-doo
farofa	fah-HOH-fah
favela	fah-VAY-lah
feijoada	fay-ZHWAH-dah
festas juninhas	FAYS-tahs zhoo-NEE^n-yahs
gaucho	GOW-shoo
Iêmanjá	yay-mah^n-SHAH
Iguaçu	ee-gwah-SOO
novela	noh-VAY-lah
Pelé	peh-LAY
Rio de Janeiro	HEE-oo dee zhah-NAY-roo
São Paulo	SOW^n POW-loo
Xuxa	SHOO-shah

46

More Books to Read

Bennett, Olivia. *A Family in Brazil.* Minneapolis: Lerner Publications Company, 1986.

Benson, Kathleen and Jim Haskins. *Count Your Way through Brazil.* Minneapolis: Carolrhoda Books, Inc., 1996.

Dawson, Zoe. *Postcards from Brazil.* Austin, TX: Raintree Steck-Vaughn Publishers, 1996.

Flora. *Feathers Like a Rainbow: An Amazon Indian Tale.* New York: HarperCollins, 1989.

Goodman, Marlene. *Let's Learn Portuguese Picture Dictionary.* Lincolnwood, IL: National Textbook, 1994.

Kent, Deborah. *Rio de Janeiro.* Danbury, CT: Children's Press, 1996.

Lewington, Anna. *Antonio's Rain Forest.* Minneapolis: Carolrhoda Books, Inc., 1993.

Papi, Liza. *Carnavalia! African-Brazilian Folklore & Crafts.* New York: Rizzoli, 1994.

Sauvain, Philip. *Rain Forests.* Minneapolis: Carolrhoda Books, Inc., 1996.

Stiles, Martha Bennett. *James the Vine Puller.* Minneapolis: Carolrhoda Books, Inc., 1992.

New Words to Find

Amazon rain forest, 6, 10−11, 12, 13

Amazon River, 6, 10

animals, 7, 10−11, 45

art, 42−43

Bonfim, 30

Carnaval, 28−29

cities, 7, 13, 16−17

crafts, 42−43

equator, 9

families, 40−41

farmers, 6, 18−19

favelas, 16−17

festivals, 28−31

food, 18−19, 38−39

gauchos, 19

Iguaçu Falls, 7

languages, 20−21

map of Brazil, 4

maracas, 27

music, 26−27

Pelé, 35

people, 12−13, 14−15, 16−17

plants, 6, 11, 44

religion, 24−25

schools, 16, 32−33

slavery, 12, 14

sports, 34−35

television, 36−37

travel methods, 22−23

weather, 8−9